A Matter of Waiting

A Matter of Waiting

Poems of My Days

PHILIP HEFNER

RESOURCE *Publications* • Eugene, Oregon

A MATTER OF WAITING
Poems of My Days

Resource Publications
An Imprint of Wipf and Stock Publishers
199 W. 8th Ave., Suite 3
Eugene, OR 97401

www.wipfandstock.com

PAPERBACK ISBN: 978-1-7252-7363-4
HARDCOVER ISBN: 978-1-7252-7364-1
EBOOK ISBN: 978-1-7252-7365-8

Manufactured in the U.S.A.   05/28/20

For Neva

Contents

INTRODUCTION

DEEP DOWN

With gratitude to Gerard Manley Hopkins.

There's a deep-downness in things,
A cantus firmus that undergirds the whole.
We lift our voices and it rings
Through the years, the very soul

Of what enables us through the toll
Of our days to journey on. Whatever
The path, the boulder we must roll
Becomes a labor of hope that may waver,

But in its rugged climb bestows a favor,
Reveals a worth and a meaning
That despite our fears will not sever
Itself from us. It is like a gleaning—

The days provide scraps of dreaming.
Even when we fear the sun will never break
Through the clouds, when victory, seeming
To be forever lost, is a thing we take

As fantasy. The scraps though small make
Us understand that dreams take root in deep
Soil. The daily flow of love and care as well leaves a wake,
A surprising freshness for us to reap,

A freshness that goes on and on—and sings.

GOD, PLAY THE BLUE GUITAR

Homage to Wallace Stevens

I.

Picasso drew the man with a blue guitar
we did not know the guitar creates a world
our green world exactly as it is
and yet beyond our world as we yearn to be

Who gets a blue guitar is every harp blue
or sole possession of the greats
reward just for masters or for everyman
is every one a maker of worlds

Do small everyday pluckers create
commensurate with their corner do they
transport their neighbors beyond
themselves with charisma that persuades

Is more required only those gifted
by the muse with consummate skills
can change our worlds
and lift them to a truer power

Poets transform the world exactly as it is
with a magic sense
and propose we give ourselves
into their grasp

Taking us to places we've not been
and when the guitar plays our green
sings it into blue we wonder where
we belong

II.

Who sings our green world blue
born to hear sermons paint a
future world in proper hue

To read a holy book "
Jesus loves me Jesus loves me
the bible tells me so

Naive no longer as to
whats green whats blue
believe with passion show

Commitment for whats true
with reasons steady gaze
eyes always upon the blue

Must oversimple ancient sage
give way to science or is the poet
more able to unfold life's wrinkled

Folds who has mastered the strings
of the blue guitar to whom
will I listen as she sings
or must I be the singer—from my tomb

III.

What is real—the guitarists blue
or the green in which I spend
my days who is the maker of
the truest song
that becomes our world

The singer sole artificer of

the world does the blue guitar
master the night and portion
out the sea is there no sea
that may defy the poet

Ice covers the lake before me
come August white caps
will race to shore
are they bluer than ice

The shrubs at my window
are barren twigs rattling in
the wind will soon be wreathed
in leaves and buds
is barren bluer than
leafy green

Singer strummer preacher
scripture or ancient sage—
or I myself—what does
it matter

I can settle for fabricated blue
but if even the green is not the green
that I've supposed

Then whats true is not the pivot
of the song ice or white caps
skeleton branches or leafy boughs
is not the choice

rather what
pleases and persuades

IV.

Whether the preacher in the collar
from the pulpit or the old blue man
with the guitar or I untutored in the song

Matters not as much as
that the music seem
a tune beyond us yet ourselves

Green enough to fit the self
we know ourselves to be
blue enough to body forth
the self that is our hope

V.

What if the guitarist
is beyond us

What if the Spirit plucks the
strings
my fingers
but the strum of the beyond
the instrument all too mortal
the music beyond mortality

Spirit within my spirit
crying now in crescendo
now pianissimo
abba abba
the hearts wish for life
resounded from us abroad
and from beyond to us

green transformed blue

not two but one

God play for me
the blue guitar

PART I

SOUL SHAPE

SOUL SHAPE

emptiness that is never vacant

the sea's immense quilt
    never at rest

      beat of the waves
      drumming like a heart
      the firmness of a pulse

endlessness of the plains
    brown paper stretching
    wherever I look
    wrapping the world
    dotted sparsely
    with lonely night lights
    blinking
    from forlorn just
    as lonely towns
    and truck stops
    their harsh lights
    absorbed by dark
    open
    ready
    empty

the call of the mesas
    breaking my heart
    in the orange and purple
    of day's end
    land of the sipapu
    whence the first people
    wend their way
    through

emptiness that is fullness
        enchanting, some say—or
        magical

depressing say others
        bereft of green
you cannot plumb
        the depths of this
        emptiness—cannot know
        a beginning or an end
        cannot reckon the beauty
holy fearsome
        alluring

these nourish my soul

        there's a starkness deep down there
        that is nurture

if at bottom there is
        divinity
        God is spare
big bang power
        galactic explosive
foundations shaking
        even as they form
never fully shaped
        shaking still
        in the power whence they
        come

dna-sprung
        energy that lures all
        moths to the flame

we were born of flame
    febrile
    labile
    to flame we are destined

God is the fire
    the shaking
    the rumble
    the whoosh

not much sentimentality there
    but fire without end
    birth everlasting
    out of the
    tremendum
    that mothers
    every living thing

light years of empty

infinity of
    possible

endless poiesis

A PARABLE

I will turn my mind to a parable,
with the harp I will solve my problem.

—PSALM 49

I.

I asked my self to reveal myself to me:
"Disclose your depths, tell me what you see."

Whether in the mirror or the eye of my mind,
I see but little; there must be more that I do not find.

II.

Myself responds: "There is yet another reflecting glass—
other selves," that live with me in the same space where I pass

my days. Jean-Paul said "hell is—
other people"—not evil, but what they tell us,

the clues they give, may mean to console
but torment us all the same. They may sketch for us a role

we're asked to play that puts us in a bind—
far different from the narrative we have in mind.

Others—with their uncertain touch—
at times they hurt too much.

Though sincerely offered, their barely
skin-deep affirmation only rarely

satisfies our ego's appetite

that after all takes no delight

in less than total love—their focus
blurred by murkiness between us.

III.

The boy with his
cowboy doll, soon to be replaced
by the pets—
white rats, pigeons and snakes.

The awkward high school teen,
the earnest college man,
who discovered girls lately,

but knew how to get an A
and prepare for what comes next.

I went to the little boy's street,
looked at his house and all its rooms.
No Aha
in those spaces.
I remember well what took place
but do not see me there.

IV.

Perhaps I am not my self at all
not a self
that could be found.

I may be a parable—
all the pieces of my life
a story to be sung.

THE KNITTER

You created every part of me,
knitting me in my mother's womb.

—PSALM 139

Knit one purl two
or is it
knit two purl one
can the knitting master
forget
get it wrong
drop a stitch

the warp and the weft
which is which
the weaver's memory
lapses for a moment

a gene here
a gene there
a nucleotide dropped
or added in
after all, there are
three billion
inside me

the sweater with a
dropped stitch
still goes on sale
as imperfect
irregular
and warms the boy
who never knows

what's dropped
never guesses
the knitter's flawed touch

so the body
with how many
one-billionths
gone askew
has yet outlived
the legendary
three score and ten
mostly unaware
of the knitter's lapse
or is it flawed
can the lost stitch
by design
have been mislaid
the genes with intent
been re-spelled
departing from
the norm
the sweater that
warms with mis-spaced
weave is a different
wrap—not flawed
so the re- or dis-
ordered As and Cs
and Gs and Ts
make a different
body, not junk
and that body's
reach is its own
sure grasp—not
an error

what did the knitter
have in mind

praise the one
who knits

This poem and the following two poems reflect on the poet's birth with
spina bifida and later years living with the consequences.

A nucleotide is a structural unit of DNA and RNA.

Nucleotides associated with DNA are commonly referred to as A, C,
G, and T. A=adenine; C=cytosine; G=guanine; T=thymine. These are
called the alphabet of the genetic code.

TO THE KNITTER

Shit!
this is your
idea of a sweater
your
design
of a body

You didn't tell me
that it would
begin
unraveling
at precisely
the place
you started
dropping stitches

This is your great idea
of a
body

Yes, I know
that I got
better than
I deserve
and what's left
works better than
ever can be justified
at four score
But still—
is
whirlwind speech
all I get
in explanation

My protest is
not Job's
nor Lear's

What would you expect
mine is what
a prissy
watered down
american christian
can muster—
an insult to
you
and
me

pathos—
where I had hoped
for tragedy

is this
your design
too

THE KNITTER RESPONDS

Do I understand you
You lament that
You're pathetic—
Ask to be tragic

Is that what you said

Tragedy

I have left your body intact
Have not cut your family to pieces

You served a life of good work
Let down gently
To a bourgeois ending

Soft—suitable to
Who you are

That epithet
Hurled at me
Leaves you strangely
Satisfied

Better I say
You
craft
A prayer of thanks

Look at Job—

You're no better, and
I destroyed him—

Genuine tragedy

"But you restored him in the end"

That is a fanciful touch
Added by a wishful
Coward

A QUESTION

When the pains began to savage me,
they became my center—
all I could think about
was how I could make them go away.

But it was I must say exciting
and in its own way that pain kept my spirit lively.

More excitement lay ahead.
Weeks and months, a long journey,
guided by doctors
seeking causes
and treatments that could
banish the hurt.

Then the weeks with therapists and trainers.
Climbing the mountains—
"Now try this"—"yes, you must do this"—
"You can do this—again and again and again."

And I could and I did.
Pain ebbed as strength returned.

Climbing those mountains was exhausting,
invigorating,
and kept me on edge.

And beyond words satisfying.

Now that I've been on that
mountain, felt the push
that took me to my limit,
the achievement has turned into

routine,
satisfaction has transformed itself
into tedium.

Must I now pray
for pain to revisit?

CHARON

what's an ugly guy like you at my door?
looks like you just
crawled up from
the swamp
hunchback
locks and all
sordid as long
and grimy

time to pick you up

me? haven' t called
haven't got the fare

but your card's been punched
a one way fare

and who punched it

ah, that's the question—
who's footing the tab?
they never say
but just send the ticket

and one way to where

this here punt of mine
only knows one place to go

does the journey end with you
or is there more

you're quite the one for quizzes

you are
but so are the others

ah i am no master
no answers
at the back of my book

it's you must get it right

GETTING IT RIGHT

styx is more a gateway
than journey's end
charon gets us started
but only that

our maker fine-tuned
this world and all its parts
its design
and we are in it
in the story lived out
in Jesus' days on earth

that story is the point
not just the trip with charon
the maker is author
has written us in
the Jesus tale

charon says my ticket's punched
more important
that ticket was punched
eighty years ago
at birth
a greater than
the hunchback boatman
has taken me on a
life long trip

i was not whole
when i came
from mother's caring body
became a fuller man
on that long journey

what's ahead
will never end
until God wraps up
all the quarks and neutrinos
that were born
of the big bang

and then i'll be
in the designer's
cosmic womb—
a universe much greater
than any of the multiverses
we might discover here

okay old man
will i need a jacket

MY SOUL THIRSTS

God, my God, you I crave;
my soul thirsts for you,
my body aches for you
like a dry and weary land.

—PSALM 63

Soul thirsting what could that
mean
or body aching like a
dry land
how does a land feel
when its weary
my soul thirsts for you, like a dry and weary land

Metaphors
its all
metaphors
painted on the sides of moving vans
in Athens
they are the carriers

What do they carry
meaning of course
we know that but
what of it

Saying metaphor
makes it seem less real
something missing
needs to be brought
from somewhere else

My soul *does* thirst
body *does ache*
I *am* that dry, baked
sun-cracked plain

For what do I thirst
for what do I ache
not water
not balm

Whatever it's for
it's my God

May my thirst be
large insatiable
let the ache be
deep unbearable

Lest my God
be too small
unworthy

MY BODY ACHES FOR YOU LIKE A
DRY AND WEARY LAND

God, my God, you I crave;
my soul thirsts for you,
my body aches for you
like a dry and weary land.

—PSALM 63

My body aches for you like a dry and weary land.
Do you take delight in my discomfort?
Is this a sadistic turn I've never seen 'til now?
Will you restore at last the bones you crush—

My body aches for you—like a dry and weary land
Always aches—cracked and baked in desert sun,
Stained by blood and greed enacted on its space.
Our lament what you made with care bent out of shape.

My body aches for you. Like a dry and weary land,
I know the rains will come, the stain transformed,
The bent reshaped, trued to its own best form.
My body, like the land, bears hope deep down.

My body aches for you like a dry and weary land.

SOUL THIRST

God, my God, you I crave;
my soul thirsts for you,
my body aches for you
like a dry and weary land.

—PSALM 63

Thirsting soul, what could that mean?
Or body aching, a dry and weary land?
When weary how does such land feel—
body and soul and agony in blend?

It's not men famished a'crawl in desert sand,
Nor woods burned out nor bodies seeking drink.
It's metaphor, in Greece, a moving van.
What's transported? Not things tangible. I think

They carry meanings—elusive misty things.
Say metaphor: it seems to me less real,
lacks touch and feel. My ache rings
body through. I am that sun-cracked plain.

A blessed state—I pray the ache wrack deep,
Since God alone, no lesser balm, will heal.

ABSURDITY

It is that kind of imperfection
through which infinity wounds the finite.
—CHRISTIAN WIMAN

If only infinity cared enough to wound.
That would be the proof enough of grace.

Grace after is all God's thereness, while
my testimony is of absence. It is too

much to say that God absconded—
God was never here.

Why would God hide in absurdity?

The deepest wound: excising
the hole into which I could descend
and search for absence.

(The opening couplet is from Christian Wiman's "Poem Ending with a Sentence from Jacques Maritain.")

COLLAGING

I like collaging because you can put things together
that shouldn't be together, and that's my life.

—CHINESE ARTIST MICHAEL CHOW,
QUOTED IN THE NEW YORK TIMES, FEBRUARY 23, 2015

Paragraphs from newspapers unrelated
wedding announcement death notice
cat caught in a tree boy caught in crossfire
as he walks to school killed by happenstance

perhaps a strip from an old shower curtain
an old phone bill odd that scraps should
crash together on my easel charming
even in their meaninglessness an artifice

boiled together in a desultory act
product of my equally desultory mind
not planned leapt at slapped together
in a moment when time hung loosely

and just meandered here and there
collage a parable of my life
try to put the days and years together
recall the boy who explored the parks

and trees and alleys of a native city
and streams and wooded colorado mountains
that live nowhere but in the imagination
of the boy now become an aging man

yet for that more real than ever

paste next to that the years where
farm land stretched as far as eye can
gaze and where a girl in a turquoise
dress with long brown hair appeared

from nowhere and never left

her sixty years ago image
glued in the old man's mind
as pleasurably imprinted now
as when it ricocheted into the brain
of that nineteen year old
and inspirited a psyche that never
recovered not calmed down to this day
there have been other cities

with no connection to the western
streams and peaks nor to the
farms and cornfields where the
turquoise girl appeared

as the new york man from china says
things put together that should
never really touch that
share so very little

thats my life

WHAT DO YOU BELIEVE ABOUT
DEATH, THE STUDENT ASKED?

Based on an actual conversation with medical students.

An obituary will say eighty-something.
That's quick and easy—
the moment
I twinkled
in two sets of eyes
up to the day the twinkle in me
dies.

It's not so easy.
I go back much farther—
the dust of stars
floats in my flesh.
Orang and Neanderthal are
my kin.

Primeval stuff
and primate
genes
do not halt their
flow because this pulse
stops.

Shattered into a thousand shards
by earth's grinding
blows
is not death
but a thousand more
openings—

paths through

cosmos, shapes as
yet unseen,
undreamt.
Who can write this obit?
Alone

one who
listens to the
whirlwind,
who hears
the voice
Job heard.

Faith
is hoping,
on the way
out,
there is a story
to be told.

GET READY

Get ready

Molecules: Get ready, my little ones,
you tiny ones—
you were not together before we met,
you will not be together much longer,
you will find new friends,
you will travel to places you do not know,
and you will be part of something
very big and new.

Memories: Never bound in time and space,
you will be even more on your own,
reaching places never imagined.
You already know how to live in contradiction,
but it will be even more intense as years pass.
You will comfort some and bring strength.
Live with the fact that you will anger others
and disappoint.

Deeds: Etched, incised,
implanted where you really matter,
freeing and imprisoning—
anonymous as you are effective.

Me, I, soul, center: How shall I name you?
You will be carried to terra truly incognita
where your life will be
novel beyond present telling.

All transported,
carried in arms
as real as they are metaphor.

PART II

WALKING THROUGH

WALKING THROUGH

Life is walking through a thicket—with no paths marked
for some, but
for others, a recreation,
a romp
in nature.

Life is walking. Through a thicket with no paths marked,
it's a challenge,
a tangle that allows an open sky,
or is it God?
but no sense of what's ahead.

Life is walking through a thicket. With no paths marked,
I find my way
just by going,
step by
step.

Life is walking through a thicket with no paths—marked
only by traces
of those who have
wandered, as I,
in times past.

Life is walking through a thicket with no paths marked.
Will my way
leave a track
for those
who make the trek after me?

Life is walking through a thicket with no paths marked.

THE MYSTERY WINKS AT YOU

Odd moments, with no regularity.
Yet any moment in our day may be

an opening into depth that tears
away the ordinary. It may bring fears

as it unfolds a more real
dimension, a veritable seal

there's more to our routine
than we have ever seen.

There's comfort in the mundane
stream of hours and days, a same-

ness that assures the fabric
of our world will hold, stick

together. We hug the surface
of life, for its familiar solace.

Mystery rewrites the rules,
requires that we bring new tools

to how we live and think—
of Mystery we can only bear a wink.

A SHADOW OF BLACKBIRDS

You forget it—sometimes
    for a long time—

It seems to journey a far distance
    but it returns reliably
    even if for only an instant

Comes between the dream
    and the actuality

Between the high charging breaker
    and the dissolving into vanishing foam

Between the open arms
    and the limp kiss

Between the satisfying recollecting
    and the pained forgetting

Flitting through the bare branches
    of the mind

Coiling in the nest of asps
    posing as familiars

The blackbirds are omens of the shadow

Shadow is silent
The birds sing

I strain to hear them sing

Even more I listen to catch

the chords that echo after the song—
innuendos that follow
the trills

The devil lives in the innuendoes

The shadows bring dark and fear
The blackbird song enters the soul
    and macerates the spirit

Shadow and blackbird
    threaten

[Shadow recalls T. S. Eliot's "The Hollow Men." Blackbirds recalls Wallace Stevens' "Thirteen Ways of Looking at a Blackbird."]

BACKSIDE

I have a longtime interest in the fronts and backs of things . . .
one is cozy, the other malign.

—Sculptor Cornelia Parker,
on her piece, *PsychoBarn*.

"One is cozy, the other malign"—
But which is which?

Something about the backside of things
That's hard to resist
Take a peek, investigate
Unveil unmask undress undo
Wonder at facades
Allow them to be awesome
See through them
Backside intended to be unpretentious
Seedy even
Messy unfinished
Taped and glued
But see deeper what's behind

Chicago facades
Gray stone frosting
Backed by common brick—
Deceiving, yes,
But not flawed for living

Potemkin's villages—
Were they myth?
Or dreams and hopes
Of a better day?

Behind each mask
Resides something—

An actor playing a role
On the stage

A charming woman
Gracing the ball

A surgeon
Cutting through
Life and death

Not every facade is a false front

KNOWING

What we did not know
was the trail westward
we the Lewis & Clark
daunting yes
demanding more from us
than we imagined
when we struck out
willing to follow
where we were led

we were blindsided
to be sure
met unexpected
trials and steep
climbs through openings
we could barely see

What we chose not to know
was another matter
it still is
it never goes away

it challenged when
and where
and how
we did not discern
and do not

worse it lamed us
it made us walk
when we should have run
flattened us
when we should have

made our way through [and
climbed still higher]

And there was also silence
what we do not know
we cannot speak of

things needed to be spoken
willing our selves ignorant
makes the silence willful
demonic
malignant

But above all
in the ignorance
and the
silence

we do not know
who we are

we lose our selves

WHAT'S THERE

disquieting
    as a premonition

gladdening
    as a hope

uncertain
    as a wish

you sense it you do
    a presence

don't you
    a thereness

as close as
    the colors in our
    eyes
    the sounds in our
    ears

these names
    don't (quite) say what we think
    we know

concepts don't cover the
    the territory

faulty words and concepts do
    remind us that

we converse poorly
    with what is there

even less hear
    its words to us

what if the there
    is a thou

a presence
    in a muted state

God hides in the thereness
    we cannot love
    (so Luther thought)

(Stevens said) the God-there
    must of necessity

hear not speak not
    since only humans
    require conversation

hope is more real
presence goes deeper
    not dependent
    on words

GRIEF

mostly silent guest
uninvited companion
shade that doesn't
want to go away
stays and overstays

baggage we don't see
but feel its weight
every day

grieving's subject
has many faces

the one

who has lived
so close
alongside and within
that apartness
is unreal

the self we used to be

the way we moved
pirouetted
ran that mile
laid a hook shot
swisher every time

the skills we had
crocheted
wielded scalpel
massaged the keys

blew reveille
and taps as well

luck
never came
openings closed
dreams—
relished for their memories
lamented their stillbornness

they say we pass through
grief's tunnel
to the light

like saying the light
will come on after we sit
in darkness

the tunnel has its own worth
it makes us
more fit—
for what?
restless agony
'til we reach
the what we do not know

I'M WATCHING

As the eyes of servants look to the hand of their master,
as the eyes of a maid to the hand of her mistress.

—PSALM 123

Eyes roving, darting—
focused every moment—
absorbing, taking it all in.
People-watching,
no end in mind,
no apology needed—
a pleasure of its own.

Looking for a face.
Lips and eyes smiling?
Hello, come near.
A latent sneer?
Stay away. A casual
indifferent glance?
Save yourself the
trouble.

Focusing on faces
that can give a clue
about what comes next—
you're tuned in, wired
for what's impending.
Lifted eyebrow, twitched
nose send a signal.

Scowl. Loaded eyes.
Lethal intent aimed right
at me. Why? What

commandment broken?
Give a nod, let your lips
shape a word that
can rescue me.

I watch for something more,
a welcome glance from surrounding hills,
inviting swish of wind in trees,
knowing nod from birds and hounds,
a cosmic smile, nothing less
than contours that conform
shape of world to feel of me.

FROM MY WINDOW

In the foreground
three-storey six-flats
and a building
ten floors high—
I see the lights come on
when darkness falls,
some stay on all night
always the same, shades
seldom down—
living high above
they feel safe
from prying eyes.

In middle range, more mid-rises
dominating the six-flats
set like checker pieces among
the trees.

In the distance, they touch the sky
—presiding over
them the great Sears Tower
Everest surrounded by
foothills of glass and stone
and steel.

A COMMONWEALTH OF EYES

A God's-eye view
of every single one
of every place
every time and space

What could that mean
not for nothing
named omniscient
God's eye is everywhere

What difference does it make
God is watching—
policeman in the sky
ready in each instant
to put his hand
into the swirl

or caring
for each of us
each time and space
protecting under warm wings

Are there many eyes
each of us a view from self
each moment
each place and space
None are blind

It's not just us and God

Each grain of sand
clod of earth
ear of corn on stalk

and bird sheltered there
from hunter's gun

houses have faces
many-eyed towers
of steel and glass
what do they see
alone and all together

We see our lofty
dreams—ready to enact
They see what our eyes
have put in place
admiring, lamenting
cheering,
crying out in pain

Egomania of our eyes
misses much

We walk
in a
commonwealth of eyes

ABSENCE

Short term absences—
they will not last—
we know that.

But absences so long
we cannot see their end—
these are
the empty moments,
the aching void,
the abyss.

Absence
brings a different way of being,
living with oneself,
whether in tranquil solitude
or in loneliness.

Absence is a teacher
of courage
and self-reliance,
or, as often,
an instructor
of despair.

Absence
prepares the soil
where I can grow
through loss
to find a deeper self.

NEW HEART

I will give you a new heart
and place a new spirit within you
taking from your bodies your stony hearts
and giving you natural hearts.
—EZEKIEL 36:26

There are the cosmic battles
armaments of the Final Solution
that win for us eternal victory

As well visions of the New
Jerusalem gold cobblestones
angels singing all the while

Not to mention hours of ease
clouds to float on a harp
to each for thrumming

There are pearly gates
to be unlocked fright'ning
bar before a judge unflapped

There's a future in each of these
a promise for everlasting days
but I will take Ezekiel

Away my heart of stone
in its place warm flesh
heart inspirited that loves and cares

INSPIRED BY TREES

In summer
your garb
of green

calms my spirit
I take you for granted

Your brightly colored
autumn hats
quicken me to attention

But in winter
bare naked
I see you truly

You are reaching
toward heaven
your stark branches
a prayer

PART III

OF PLIGHT AND PAIN

THE SHAPE OF TRUTH

When the chips are down, where does truth stand?
Does it sketch the contours, the lay of the land?
Does truth like the judge in the court set forth the rules?
Does it stand aloof, our struggles just the work of fools?

Or with humorless prosecutor's bite,
will it press itself upon us until we get it right,
allowing no shades of meaning, but like a hound,
pursue with no relenting until we fall to ground?

Truth is a plea—taking our defense with passion.
We seek a proper way, often against the fashion
of the wider path, where men of wealth and power
hold successful cards and bask in fame's shower

of acclaim. Against prevailing winds that overturn
our craft, truth remains loyal, through waves that churn
before the fragile vessel in which we stand.
Truth stays with us even when the fearsome band

of falsehood's shameless horde seems to gain
the upper hand. Truth may come as gentle rain
as often as it wields the sure swift sword of wrath.
Truth may stay unseen, though always present on our path—

not one to flaunt itself in garish garb, or parade
with boastful swagger. While liars practice their charade,
though it may seem weak, even dead upon the ground,
truth knows resurrection and will go for yet another round.

POETIC THEMES

must be chosen with care these days
beauty redefined
angst of heart enlarged
order and reason conceived and
shaped anew

the times when living rhymes with dying
oblige poets to walk a different road

> Chorus One: "workers be damned, it's profits
> that count!" "We never meant to pay a living wage,
> we just offer a chance to work!"

money, profits that's what counts
not a thing of beauty
no grace there—
for single mom
high school dropout
anyone down on their luck

never meant as living wage
job may not rhyme with life but
we wish you well

> Chorus Two: "new law mandating retirement
> pension for every worker? Just another assault on
> American business!" A screed well known today.

you didn't get it?
making profit is what it's all about—
transform that into iambs
with sustaining cadence
go ahead if you can

Chorus Three: "I can't breathe!" "Hands up! don't
shoot" insults every man and woman with a badge
disrespects those who serve and protect.

insult how terrible
for darren and eric and sean and amidou
tamir twelve years old with toy gun
a man of ninety-two name unknown
mindless in a nursing home
it was their last sigh
now at rest beneath the earth
it offends you when we
remember

Chorus Four: "When all the facts are in you
will surely understand why no shooter need
stand trial need defend their deed."

gun culture embedded
to our core have a gun shoot
kill
your supreme
service
and protection

american as god and mother
(used to be)

Chorus Five: Players protest, "Hands up, don't
shoot." "We draw a line. Who buys the stuff you
advertise? It's us, cops, the good people. If you
don't stop, we'll step in."

what serves these times best

ode sonnet rhymed or free
epic lament or dirge

these are ordered forms
the times shatter form

are poems real in this time
is this a poem

if not poem what

king gandhi jesus
their lives are poems
epic sagas

their lives are also
deaths defying
meter and rhyme

ours is
the age
after poetry

AN IMAGE PROBLEM

In mid-September, 2014, several professional
football players were charged with assault
on women and children.

He hit her—hard
a greek god in
perfect shape
no problem dragging her
unconscious body
from the elevator

What's the issue here
an image problem say
the pundits says the
league say the
lawyers

Dollars, where do
they fit in

He's an all-star they say
They're a loving couple
they say

He pulls in the dollars
they say

Adonis beats the
little boys who adore him
welts and scars that
last forever

We've got an image problem here

to be sure

Whupped him like
my daddy did to me
made me a better person
another says

Dollars must be safe
a bottom line belief

Running is his game
and he's good at it
record books prove it

An image problem
no right and wrong
here

Forget the women
sent by the blows
into oblivion
made up now in
black and blue

Dismiss the boys
they're on their way
to becoming better men
they bear not scars
so much as badges
of spiritual forming

Run, run, run

At all costs, keep
the silver coming in

safe always
dollars always safe

this is America's game

OTHERING

So many ways to say we're other
    different clans, not my tribe
    not normal, don't look like me
    not conforming, don't act like us
    dangerous, don't believe like me

We have special words
    undocumented
    goy
    gayjin
    leper
    them, not us

We have special ways to act
    put you on a reservation
    offer bad schools
    make you move out
    beat you into senselessness
    make you use a different bathroom
    lynch you
    gun you down
    je suis Orlando
    je suis Omar

So few ways to say
    we belong
    we're one
    we're family

Let me try

Started out
    in the same

Big Bang
     stardust every one
Clambered out
     of the primeval soup
     as one

Shinnied up the
     tree of life
     together,
     absorbed the same
     Chimpanzee stock

Migrated out of Africa
     together refugees
     from the Savannah

The same good God
     breathed life
     into our clay
     in the image of that God
     family

We fell into otherness
     just as early
     already as Chimps
     tribes came easily to us

But family must come first

Slave galley
Wounded Knee
Stonewall
Mother Emanuel
Orlando

This necessary litany of blood and shame

Must transmute
    othering
    into
    family celebration

WHEN DOES THE WAR END?

When does the war end?
Remembering a cousin
Short and stocky,
He bounced when he walked.
Forearms as big as Dempsey's,
Whose twelve inch punch
Could crush a man's skull.

"You ought to be a boxer,"
His uncles urged.

Guadalcanal in November
Nineteen forty-two
Changed things.

The bow of his ship,
The New Orleans,
Blown apart in the Battle of
Tessofaronga—sweet-sounding
Name of the burial waters
Where hundreds of boys—
Navy men—lie sleeping.

A miracle, the doctors
Told him. "Your life's been
Spared." The shrapnel that
Crashed into his eye
Never reached his brain.
But it left a hole.

That wasn't the end of Leo's war.
He never sailed a battle cruiser
Again, but his war

Went on and on.

On Armistice Day, back home,
Parades celebrated on Colfax Avenue
And on every Main Street in America.
Mayors and senators and the President
And generals and admirals declared
"Peace is here, War is over."
We cheered and waved our hands
Holding American flags.
Leo's war continued.
He fought the ghosts that haunted
His days and nights. Searched for
Love he never found.
At the end, runaway cancer cells
Found him.
With ninety proof meds
His daily portion,
He fought for fifty years.
His war never ended.
He stopped fighting.

BRING ME A LIPSTICK

Response of a woman during the siege
of Sarajevo, February 1996, when a journalist
asked what she should bring on her next visit.

I saw the red of flowing blood
and committed to bringing bandages

when brown earth exploded in my face
I knew I must plant a garden

silver missiles shattering my nights
filled my eyes with unnatural light
persuaded me to paint beautiful images

I scrub my face clean put on clothes
that are whole—no rags or tears

I sing my songs, fearing
war's silences more than the bombs

I dance to save my soul—
the most terrible casualty imaginable

my soul is that of a woman
and I stand for life

I give birth I teach beauty and joy
and caring and planting and healing

bring me a lipstick
I want that sniper
when he lifts his gun
to see that he

takes aim at a
beautiful woman

WILD LIGHTS

Thoughts while seeing
an ambulance parked at
the front entrance.

frenetic frantic flashing lights
unsettling me nervous jumping lights
we're in a hurry to move
krankenwagen lights

in the night
there's a wildness
about those lights
a deer frozen in place
yet wanting to flee
wildness

in a sheltered spot
porte cochere softens
the storm for you
as you enter
to be driven now with
piercing screams
away

i do not want you to go
this night
alone
i am in the wagon
with you
into the wild

CAN'T SLEEP/WON'T SLEEP/MUSTN'T SLEEP

Can't sleep—
4 a.m. awake, mind rushing
two more days
surgeon's scalpel cuts out
runaway cells
in precise jargon they say
"undifferentiated invasive ductal carcinoma"
    masks the terror
    deepens the terror
    makes it more awful
more than awake
beyond unsettled mind
nausea—losing it
losing heart
losing reason altogether
one with you who may be losing all
never closer than now
to you who may be losing all

Won't sleep
keep watch with you
are you asleep
to sleep is to betray you
to say I don't care—I do care
I can shake this off—I can't
sleep is a lie

Mustn't sleep
need to know
the foe
the pain
the life not yet about to go
not yet letting go

must never sleep again
whether you let go now
or never let go
a witness must stand
an obelisk raised up
testimony etched
in lids never closed
sleeplessness
sleep held at bay forever

STICKLES

Paining hip stickles my brain
aching tooth vies for attention

My spirit does not hurt so much
It grieves
what has been lost
Pain pales
as spirit feels the absent vigor
that no longer drives the limbs

What is spirit
that it can referee
the contest of pain and loss
Is it more than hip and tooth
sovereign over body

Or body in a different way of being
body defying its fate
containments
labels
predictions
defining body in unexpected ways

Play on tooth and hip
I watch your twisting moves
listen to your grunts
My spirit attunes
a larger confrontation
a deeper sense of
what body is about
There's more at stake
by far than your
skin-deep rant

Your duel goes on and on
I go my own way
not settling for the options
you offer
Like Jacob ever marked
yet redefined and free

COTTON AT MUSEUM OF CONTEMPORARY ART

inspired by the exhibit of Virgil Abloh

White on Black
Black on White

Cotton boll soft and white
against the calloused black hands
that picked it

black hands and aching black backs
within the white world
that lived off black backs

Cotton Incorporated
a world perpetuated
still white

I feel most black when I am
against a white background
I feel most white when I am
against a black background

[with respects to Zora Neale Hurston]

A LOVER'S MIND

One must have a lover's mind to truly see the world.

One must have a lover's mind to truly see the world,
else all will seem
as offal
from a process misbegotten,
a miserable grind best forgotten.

One must have a lover's mind. To truly see the world,
to pierce through obfuscating
layers—
we must form a conception
that allows for genuine affection.

One must have a lover's mind to truly see. The world
does not open to us easily.
It holds itself together tightly.
When we seek its secrets to unspool,
we find empathy is a most useful tool.

One must have a lover's mind to truly see the world
as more than enigmatic and
cruel.
"Nothing in the world, nothing human is alien to me"—
If we want to know the world truly, that is the key.

One must have a lover's mind to truly see the world.

FINALE

A MATTER OF WAITING

I.

There comes a moment
    when it's a matter of waiting.
Not a moment of inactivity
    or a diminishing of creativity.
But nevertheless a time when you
    know, with an awareness in the
    background, that you are waiting for
    something to happen, for someone to appear.

It matters not what one is waiting for,
    what the event is.
It may be a sensitive, friendly guide
    for a trip to a new, unfamiliar
    place.
Or the appearance of a breathtaking choir,
    divine singing fronted by horns—
    trumpets mainly, accompanied by
    trombones and drum rolls.
Or again, perhaps a falling to sleep to dreams
    of a green-as-a-meadow future,
    Christina's yearning-yet-at-peace,
    wrapped in sleep.
Or a simple silence that does not end.

The point is, whatever or whoever
    arrives, it is a waiting.

II.

Some say that we live towards our death,
    as if death were rushing at us,

each moment demanding heroic
acts that establish once again our
inner self.

Dying is yet a metaphor,
a stand in for committing to a cause
whose demands require
that we extend ourselves with
no holding back.

These spend themselves without
surcease. They reckon their lives
in miles run, forces resisted,
energy depleted,
days and months, the interval
between the dreaming and the acting
and the end result. They know that
outcomes are too obscure; after giving all
they live in grays, founding fathers and
slaves together.

Where is the death? In spending self without
reserve, in the uncertainty of attainment
or living with the blur at the end?

Charging heroically toward death is not
measuring our lives in coffee spoons
but it is still a waiting of its own.

III.

Aged by relentless sun
beaten this way and that by
rhythms hot and cold—
boards unpainted gray and porous,

barely held in place by rusted nails—

groaning and creaking, each step echoes,
    wind squeaks
    through gaps and cracks.

This house, nearly abandoned, is
    testimony to the spirit that still
    inhabits its lonely spaces and
    yet reminder of the soul that
    left some time ago.

It stands as invitation to those who
    stop to step inside, even children
    like this one, whose feet
    echo in the house they
    once knew as home and where
    mothers' voices, overlaid by generations,
    counsel caution to exuberance that
    runs and teases.

It must be honored, granted
    landmark standing, before it
    disappears into tufts of grass
    and remnants of a foundation that
    no longer supports anything
    except that still unyielding sun
    and that unhurried tempo of
    heat and cold.

It will be a place of barrenness
    except for those who remember.

Barrenness does not happen in an instant.
    It requires moments of waiting.

And time for children to enjoy.

IV.

The moment of waiting can be sweet,
    holding within its passage
    a grace deep down,
    its stillness an aloe
    that soothes the foreboding
    and the spasm.

Grace descending like rain on the meadow,
    like raindrops on the earth.

Reminding us that the moment
    is not prelude
    not dispensable.

A necessary interlude
    between metaphor and the indescribable.

Entr'acte, one might say,
    ushering us into the age
    when dying is
    no longer metaphor.

THE PHILOSOPHER'S REPORT

"The truth is so unclear,
our time on earth so short"—
the philosopher's report
in brief describes with near
precision what frustrates
the quest that makes us who we
are—to know with certainty
and properly respect our fates.

Yet along a path we walk,
free in spirit when the way allows,
oft constrained by circumstance.
As if the path itself could talk—
in its own strange way it shows
our life's a not unpretty dance.

www.ingramcontent.com/pod-product-compliance
Lightning Source LLC
LaVergne TN
LVHW021613080426
835510LV00019B/2546